PENGUIN

TAGORE: THE WO

RABINDRANATH TAGORE (1861–1941) was one of the key figures of the Bengal Renaissance. He started writing at an early age, and by the turn of the century had become a household name in Bengal as a poet, a songwriter, a playwright, an essayist, a short story writer and a novelist. In 1913 he was awarded the Nobel Prize for Literature for his verse collection *Gitanjali*. Around the same time, he founded Visva-Bharati, a university located in Santiniketan near Kolkata. Called the 'Great Sentinel' of modern India by Mahatma Gandhi, Tagore steered clear of active politics, but is famous for returning the knighthood conferred on him as a gesture of protest against the Jallianwala Bagh massacre in 1919.

Tagore was a pioneering literary figure, renowned for his ceaseless innovations in poetry, prose, drama, music and painting, which he took up late in life. His works include some sixty collections of verse, novels like *Gora*, *Chokher Bali* and *Ghare Baire*, plays like *Raktakarabi* and *Dakghar*, dance dramas like *Shyama*, *Chandalika* and *Chitrangada*, over a hundred short stories, essays on religious, social and literary topics, and over 2500 songs, including the national anthems of India and Bangladesh.

SUGATA BOSE is the Gardiner Professor of history at Harvard University. He was educated at Presidency College, Kolkata, and the University of Cambridge where he obtained his PhD and was later a fellow of St Catharine's College. Before taking up the Gardiner Chair at Harvard in 2001, he was professor of history and diplomacy at Tufts University. Bose was a recipient of the Guggenheim Fellowship in 1997 and gave the G.M. Trevelyan Lecture at the University of Cambridge.

Bose's many books include *The Nation as Mother and Other Visions of Nationhood*, the much-acclaimed *A Hundred Horizons: The Indian Ocean in the Age of Global Empire* and *His Majesty's Opponent: Subhas Chandra Bose and India's Struggle against Empire*. He has also made documentary films on South Asian history and politics and published recordings of his translations of Tagore.

TAGORE
The World Voyager

RABINDRANATH TAGORE

Translated by SUGATA BOSE

Foreword by Former Hon. President of India,
PRANAB MUKHERJEE

PENGUIN BOOKS
An imprint of Penguin Random House

PENGUIN BOOKS

USA | Canada | UK | Ireland | Australia
New Zealand | India | South Africa | China

Penguin Books is part of the Penguin Random House group of companies
whose addresses can be found at global.penguinrandomhouse.com

Published by Penguin Random House India Pvt. Ltd
4th Floor, Capital Tower 1, MG Road,
Gurugram 122 002, Haryana, India

Penguin
Random House
India

First published by Random House India 2012
Published in Penguin Books by Penguin Random House India 2021

Translation copyright © Sugata Bose 2012

All rights reserved

10 9 8 7 6 5 4 3 2 1

ISBN 9780143453437

Typeset in Venetian301 BT by SÜRYA, New Delhi
Printed at Replika Press Pvt. Ltd, India

www.penguin.co.in

CONTENTS

SONGS IN FIVE GENRES

PREM (LOVE)

PUJA (DEVOTION)

PRAKRITI (NATURE)

SWADESH (PATRIOTISM)

BICHITRA (VARIETY)

FOREWORD

Rabindranath Tagore (1861–1941) was India's greatest gift to world culture and civilization in the late nineteenth and early twentieth centuries. Many facets of his creative genius are well known to the outside world through translations. However, his songs, which are cherished in every Bengali home, are not familiar to readers and audiences beyond Bengal and India.

Through Prof. Sugata Bose's fresh poetic translations, that are accompanied by recordings on five CDs, we now hope to reach Tagore's music to a wider audience. This special set of one book and five CDs have both readings of the English translations and the original Bengali songs. It is supported by the National Implementation Committee for the 150th birth anniversary of Rabindranath Tagore and the Ministry of Culture of the Government of India.

The book is divided into two parts. The first part titled 'Oceanic Songs' takes readers on sea journeys with Tagore between 1912 and 1934. Rabindranath Tagore's overseas voyages included visits to England and the United States in 1912–13, Japan and the United States in 1916, Europe in 1921, China and Japan in 1924, Latin America (Argentina) in 1924–25, Europe in 1926, Southeast Asia in 1927, Europe and the United States in 1930, Iran and Iraq in 1932, and Ceylon in 1934. During several of these trips Tagore composed forty songs, all of which are offered in this special gift set, along with the contexts in which each song was written.

The eleven songs composed on his voyage to England in 1912–13 will provide insights into Tagore's creativity in the domain of music just on the eve of his winning the Nobel Prize for Literature. It is interesting to note that Tagore composed as many as twenty-two songs in Germany and other countries of Central and Eastern Europe during his trip in 1926. The voyage to Latin America in 1924 and Southeast Asia in 1927 also yielded what became some of his most famous songs.

Since Tagore composed the overwhelming majority of his songs in India, the second part titled 'Songs in Five Genres' gives readers and listeners a broader sample of his creativity as a song-writer and music composer.

We are proud to share with the world at large an aspect of Tagore's genius that has been treasured in his homeland.

New Delhi,   PRANAB MUKHERJEE
December, 2011   Chairman,
                        National Implementation Committee

INTRODUCTION

'As a Bengali, I know,' Satyajit Ray said emphatically, 'that as a composer of songs, Tagore has no equal, not even in the West—and I know Schubert and Hugo Wolf.'[1]

An immensely versatile creative genius—a poet, novelist, short-story writer, playwright, composer of dance dramas, essayist, and painter—Rabindranath Tagore is best remembered in Bengal as a songwriter. Yet there is a widespread conviction among Tagore scholars—often citing contradictory reasons—that Tagore's songs are untranslatable. According to Krishna Dutta and Andrew Robinson, 'unless one can understand the words of Tagore's songs, they quickly begin to sound monotonous—though a small selection, carefully made, is usually convincing of his melodic gifts and its range'.[2] In the view of William Radice, 'Tagore expressed his romantic and religious perception most profoundly in his songs,' but they could not be rendered in translation. 'I do not think it impossible,' he wrote, 'that Tagore's songs will

---

[1]Quoted in Krishna Dutta and Andrew Robinson, *Rabindranath Tagore: The Myriad-Minded Man* (London: Bloomsbury, 1995), p. 359.

[2]Ibid.

one day be known and appreciated outside India . . . but they will have to be known as songs. Translation of the words will not be enough.'[3]

The unique blend of words and melody of Tagore's songs cannot, of course, be replicated in another language and musical culture. However, we believe with Satyajit Ray that one can discern a range of songs in which Tagore's 'poetic skills' have enhanced 'the beauty of the song, to generate an interplay of word, mood, and beat'.[4] A skilful, rhythmic translation of words and mood in these instances can capture some of the richness of Tagore's songs. Besides, it would be a mistake to preserve a wall of separation between Tagore's poems and songs. Several of his poems were set to music and are today celebrated as songs.

'Songs,' Tagore wrote in *The Diary of a Westward Voyage*,[5] 'are entirely the play of creation. As the rainbow appears, like the magic formation of rain and sun, a built-up archway of two whimsical temperaments in the sky, an exquisite moment proceeds on its triumphal journey through this very archway. In an instant the play is over, the moment passes by waving its coloured garment; there is nothing more! Song-poems are nothing but this temperamental play of colour. If the poet of the rainbow were accosted and asked, "What is one to make

---

[3]Rabindranath Tagore, *Selected Poems*, translated by William Radice (Harmondsworth: Penguin, 1985), pp. 30–31.

[4]Satyajit Ray, 'Rabindrasangite Bhabbar Katha', *Sharadiya Ekshan*, 1967, cited in Dutta and Robinson, *Rabindranath Tagore*, p. 360.

[5]Rabindranath Tagore, *Diary of a Westward Voyage* (*Pashchim Jatrir Diary*, trans. by Indu Dutt, Westport, CT: Greenwood, 1975).

out from all this?" the reply one would meet with would be, "Nothing!" "Then?" "It just pleases me!"—the pleasure of the pure form, to every challenge, to creation, this is the last answer.'[6]

Tagore once told the British writer Edward Thompson, in the early 1920s: 'I have introduced some new element in our music, I know ... This is a parallel growth to my poetry. Anyhow, I love this aspect of my activity. I get lost in my songs, and then I think that these are the best of my works; I get quite intoxicated. I often feel that, if all my poetry is forgotten, my songs will live with my countrymen ... it is nonsense to say that music is a universal language. I should like my music to find acceptance, but I know this cannot be, at least not till the West has had time to study and learn to appreciate our music. All the same, I know the artistic value of my songs. They have great beauty. Though they will not be known outside my province ... I leave them as a legacy.'[7]

The ambition of this project is to convey the artistic value of Tagore's songs beyond the limits of his province, and therefore this creative combination of text and accompanying CDs.

The book is organized in two parts. The first part, titled 'Oceanic Songs', sets Tagore's musical compositions in the context of his overseas voyages between 1912 and 1934. This literary device has the advantage of introducing the lyrics and tunes of the songs to a foreign audience through a narrative of Tagore's travels during which he

---

[6]Ibid., p. 62.

[7]Edward Thompson, *Rabindranath Tagore: Poet and Dramatist* Delhi: Oxford University Press, 1992, p. 61.

communicated with the wider world. Some of the songs are inspired by specific foreign locations at sea or on land. Others simply evoke a sense of nostalgia for the homeland he left behind and a few, such as 'This jewelled chain is not for me' composed in August 1913 or 'All the wounds, as many losses' in November 1926, are a reflection of the poet's mental state in response to fame and criticism in distant lands.

Fascinating as they are, Tagore wrote only forty of his nearly 2,500 songs on his journeys abroad. To give a fuller sense of his lyrical and musical repertoire, the second part of the book presents a selection of 'Songs in Five Genres', following the generally accepted classification of Tagore's songs into the four categories of prem (love), puja (devotion), prakriti (nature), swadesh (patriotism), and the untranslatable residual category termed bichitra (variety). The songs of devotion include some that are different from the austere devotionalism of his *Gitanjali* (1912–13) phase. It is usually difficult to distinguish between Rabindranath's songs of devotion and songs of love. Far from being an other-worldly mystic, Rabindranath loved this land with a passion. Nothing reveals this more emphatically than his rich range of songs on different seasons, especially the monsoon.

Tagore's patriotism never allowed the spark of the individual to be extinguished by the collective. The final lines of one of his most memorable patriotic songs bear this out:

If no one raises a lamp, O Unfortunate,
If on dark stormy nights they shut their doors on you—
Then in the fire of lightning
Lighting up the ribs on your chest, shine on alone.

'India's learning had once spread outside India,' Tagore wrote in July 1927 as he journeyed towards Southeast Asia across the Bay of Bengal, '[b]ut the people outside accepted it ... We have embarked on this pilgrimage to see the signs of the history of India's entry into the universal.'[8] This book aims to reach Tagore's songs to people beyond the borders of India, transcending the barriers of language on the wings of music. It will enable the realization of Tagore's aspiration of spreading India's culture to distant lands around the globe:

Aji ami tare dekhi labo
Bharater je mahima tyag kori asiachhe apon anganseema
Arghya dibo tare
Bharat bahire tabo dware.

Today I will bear witness to India's glory
that transcended its own boundaries
I will pay it homage
outside India at your door.

SUGATA BOSE

[8]Quoted in Sugata Bose, *A Hundred Horizons: The Indian Ocean in the Age of Global Empire* (Cambridge, MA: Harvard University Press, 2006), p. 245.

OCEANIC SONGS

THE EXUBERANCE OF LIFE

(*PRAN BHARIYE TRISHA HORIYE*)

On June 4, 1912, Rabindranath Tagore wrote as *The City of Glasgow* sailed through the Red Sea, 'This morning as I stood on the deck holding the railing, a mild, cool breeze blew in from the west through the gap between the pale blue of the sky and deep blue of the ocean.' The poet felt that it was a blessing of His grace issuing a call from different directions of the universe with no end, no end anywhere, just more, more, and more. On June 3, just a day earlier, Tagore had composed this song:

Fill my heart, quench my thirst,
Grant me the exuberance of life.
In your universe, your mansion,
Give me a spacious abode.
More light, more light,
Pour light into these eyes, O Lord,
Fill my flute with divine tunes,
Grant me a flood of melodies.
More sorrow, more anguish,
Awake me to consciousness, O Lord,
Open doors, break down barriers,

Rescue me, grant me deliverance.
More love, more love,
Let my ego be drowned.
In a torrent of nectar
Give more, more, more of your Self.

BEAUTIFUL, TRULY, IS YOUR BRACELET

(*SUNDAR BOTE TABA ANGADKHANI*)

On June 16, 1912, Tagore reached London. After a few days he rented a house in Hampstead for his sojourn. The stunning natural beauty of Hampstead Heath was the setting for the composition of this song on June 25, 1912:

Beautiful, truly, is your bracelet, studded with stars—
In gold and jewels it is enticing, I know, in myriad colours.
Your scimitar is more gorgeous, drawn in a quiver of lightning,
Garuda's wing crimson-tinged against the setting sun in the sky.
Like life's last gasp on the verge of death, a dazzling deep anguish—
Scorches in a flash all I possess in an intense, terrifying awakening.
Beautiful, truly, is your bracelet, studded with stars,
Your scimitar, O Lord of Thunder, is the ultimate, forged in a terrible
*   beauty.*

4

INFINITE IS YOUR WEALTH

(ASHIM DHON TO AACHHE TOMAR)

Another ten months went by. After spending nearly six months in the United States, Tagore returned to London in April 1913. The 750 copies of *Gitanjali* published by the India Society of London, while he was away in America, had sold out. Macmillan had recently published a popular edition. The artist William Rothenstein, who had introduced the poet to European poets in 1912, wrote to Tagore: 'When you last came, it was as a stranger, with only our unworthy selves to offer our friendship. Now you come as a widely recognized poet and seer, with friends known and unknown, in a hundred homes.'

Away from the buzz around his newly won fame, Tagore composed three songs on August 24, 1913. He was then recuperating in a house on Cheyne Walk in Chelsea after a surgery. The songs capture the play between the finite and the infinite, and the divine presence in human existence.

Infinite is your wealth, yet unsatisfied,
You wish to receive it from my hands in tiny particles.
With your finest jewels you have made me rich—
Now you have come to my door and I have kept it shut.

You will make me munificent and you the mendicant—
The whole universe bursts out in uproarious laughter.
You will not ride that chariot, but descend to the dusty path,
You will walk by my side through ages and ages.

I WILL UTTER YOUR NAME

(*TOMARI NAAM BOLBO*)

The Upanishads had urged an occasional departure from the learned intellect to simple realization. Inspired by the ancient Indian text, there seems to be a mild echo of Robert Browning's 'The Boy and the Angel' in this song:

I will utter your name under many pretences,
Sitting alone under the shadow of my thoughts.
Say it without words, say it without hope,
Say it with my smile, say it in tears.
Without purpose I will call your name,
And fulfil needlessly my heart's desire.
Like a child enchanted by the mother's name,
Feels the bliss of saying 'Mother'.

THIS JEWELLED CHAIN IS NOT FOR ME

(*E MONIHAAR AMAY NAHI SAJE*)

Tagore wrote in a letter at this time that he felt uncomfortable about the publicity surrounding his name. Fame engendered a conflict within him. He was hurt by indifference and yet found recognition to be oppressive. He wrote to Rothenstein: 'I am pining for the touch of life, for the warmth of reality—and that is the reason why the call of my Bolpur School is getting to be more and more insistent.' It was in this frame of mind that he wrote this song:

This jewelled chain is not for me,
It is painful to wear, wounds me as I struggle to tear it off.
It stifles my voice, silences my melodies,
Distracts my mind from my work.
That is why I am waiting,
If only I could offer you this necklace, I would be saved.
Accept me, bind me to you with a garland of flowers,
I cannot show you my face, shamed by this string of gems.

AT DAWN *AND* A STORM OF JOY

(*BHORER BELAY* AND *PRANE KHUSHIR TUPHAN UTHECHHE*)

Tagore suddenly decided he would return to India in September 1913. His friends Ernest and Grace Rhys arranged a farewell dinner on August 26. Describing the event, Tagore's son Rathindranath wrote to Mrs Maycee Seymore: 'Last week some of Father's friends gave a farewell dinner to him in a restaurant in town. Mr Yeats spoke most intimately—he said that what had affected him most, and what he had never dreamed he would find in contemporary literature, was the spontaneity of poetic and spiritual feeling and expression in Father's writings.' The two songs composed by Tagore the day before, on August 25, are evidence of that spontaneity of expression.

AT DAWN

(*BHORER BELAY*)

When did you come at dawn and touch me with a smile.
Pushing the door of my sleep who brought this news,
On waking I find my eyes have been flooded with tears.
I feel as if the sky has whispered in my ear.
I feel my entire being has been filled to the brim with songs.
My heart has blossomed like flowers offered at worship wet with dew,
The river of life has broken its banks and spread to the land of infinity.

A STORM OF JOY

(PRANE KHUSHIR TUPHAN UTHECHHE)

A storm of joy has risen in my heart.
The barrier of fearful doubt is broken.
My heart ventures out today
To hold grief in a firm embrace.
I had thought there would be not enough space,
But breaking down the doors all have gathered.
I who had with care kept myself clean and pure
Roll in the dust in ecstasy.

WHEN LIFE WAS LIKE A FLOWER

(*JIBAN JAKHAN CHHILO PHULER MATO*)

The day after the farewell dinner, on August 27, 1913, Tagore wrote to C.F. Andrews: 'This morning I am going to take a motor ride to Rothenstein's country house.' There, in Far Oakridge, Gloucestershire, Tagore wrote the final song of his English sojourn.

When life was like a flower
It had hundreds of petals.
In its springtime of giving
It would shed a few leaves
And yet so much was left.
Now laden with fruit
It has nothing much left to give.
In autumn its time has ebbed
It will give of itself in full measure,
Drooping with its burden of sweetness.

SET MY LIFE TO MUSIC

(*BAJAO AMAARE BAJAO*)

On September 4, 1913, Tagore set off from Liverpool on the ship *City of Lahore*. From Gibraltar he wrote to Rothenstein that he was spending his days in peace having found a quiet corner on the deck. No one disturbed him 'except a missionary who takes every opportunity of impressing upon my mind the superiority of Christianity over Hinduism'. Tagore transcended his irritation with this competition between religions through his songs. On September 14, in the middle of the Mediterranean Sea, he appealed to the Almighty to make him an instrument of the divine.

Set my life to music
Play your melody of the light at dawn in my life.
The tune that fills your wordless songs, and a child's flute of life
Smiling at its mother's face—make me the instrument of that tune.
Adorn me,
Adorn me in the dress that adorns the dust of this earth.
The rhythmic beauty of the evening malati, adorned in its secret aroma,
The decoration that joyfully forgets itself, embellish me in that adornment.

I KNOW, THIS DAY WILL PASS

(*JANI JANI GO DIN JABE*)

On Sepetmber 18, sailing down the Red Sea, Tagore composed this wistful song:

I know, this day will pass.
At day's end the faint sun with a wan smile
Will give me the glance of a final farewell.
The flute will play by the wayside, by the riverbank cows will graze,
Children will play in the yard, birds will sing.
Yet, this day will pass.
I beg of you
Let me know before I go why I had received a call
The green earth's eyes raised towards the sky.
Why did the stillness of night utter the words of the stars,
Why did the day's light raise a flutter in my heart,
This I would beg of you.
When my turn on this earth ends
May I reach tranquillity as I finish my song,
My basket filled with the harvest of six seasons.
May I see you in the light of this life,
Place my garland around your neck,
When my turn on this earth ends.

NO CHARMING DALLIANCE

(*NOY NOY MADHUR KHELA*)

On September 19, 1913, in his last song of this long voyage, Tagore reflects on the paradox of divine love and human suffering.

No, no, this is no charming dalliance,
You and I, morning and evening, all life long
No charming dalliance is this.
So many times the light has gone out, the stormy night has come roaring,
Rocking the swing of life with doubt.
Again and again sweeping floods have burst the banks.
In dreadful times cries of lament have rent all directions.
O Destroyer, in grief and joy, my heart has learnt this lesson,
There are painful blows in your love, but never neglect.

14

YOUR UNIVERSE-ENCOMPASSING
PRAYER MAT

(BHUBAN JORA ASHANKHANI)

While the First World War raged in Europe and West Asia,
Rabindranath Tagore set off on a global oceanic voyage
from Calcutta on May 3, 1916, aboard the Japanese ship
Tosamaru. Tagore was travelling on this easterly route for the
first time in his life. His ship encountered a mighty storm in
the Bay of Bengal that left no dividing line between the
clouds and the waves. Someone seemed to have opened the
blue lid of the ocean and countless demons emerged from
below wrapped in grey coils of smoke, as in the *Arabian Nights*,
and shot up towards the sky.

After four days at sea, the appearance of birds in the sky
signalled that land was near. If the ocean was the domain of
dance, its shores heralded a realm of music. As the ship
moved up the Irrawady towards Rangoon, Tagore observed
the row of kerosene oil factories with tall chimneys along its
banks as if Burma was lying on its back and smoking a cigar.
From Burma the *Tosamaru* travelled further east towards
Penang, Singapore, and Hong Kong. It was in the midst of
another frightening storm in the South China Sea on
May 21, 1916, that Tagore composed this song asking
the Almighty to spread his seat of universality in the
individual's heart.

Your universe-encompassing prayer mat
Spread it out in the core of my heart.
The night's stars, the day's sun, all the shades of darkness and light,
All your messages that fill the sky,
Let them find their abode in my heart.
May the lute of the universe
Fill the depths of my soul with all its tunes.
All the intensity of grief and joy, the flower's touch, the storm's touch—
Let your compassionate, auspicious, generous hands
Bring into the core of my heart.

UNMINDFUL

(*ANMONA*)

In May 1924, Tagore received an invitation to attend the centenary of Peru's independence in South America. Although in poor health, Tagore set off from Calcutta on September 19, 1924. 'But the boons he received from the goddess of poetry in his tired frame,' writes Prabhat Kumar Mukhopadhyay with no exaggeration, 'will remain immortal in the history of literature; these were *Purabi* in poetry and *Pashchim Jatrir Diary* (*Diary of a Westbound Traveller*) in prose.'

On October 11, 1924, the *Harana Maru* arrived in Marseilles. After spending a week in France the poet set off for Latin America from Cherbourg. The *Andes* did not offer the same warmth of hospitality as the Japanese vessel *Harana Maru*, but Tagore discovered that it was possible to let the poetic imagination fly even inside a cramped cabin. The three-week voyage across the Atlantic afforded time for twenty-three poems. The first of these was 'Stranger' ('Aparichita') that struck a rather plaintive note on the sorrow of the poet's solitude. On the same day he composed this song:

O Unmindful,
I will not bring you the garland of my tidings.
My message will be in vain, when will I win your trust,
Your mood is inscrutable, O Unmindful.

If the time is propitious on a sweet silent evening,
Your eyes absorbed in the dim twilight,
I will offer you the solace of my tranquil melody.
I will then whisper to you my rhythm-patterned words
In a soft and gentle strain,
Just as the cricket in the sal grove on a sleepy silent night
Composes its melodious drone on the rosary beads of darkness,
Alone sitting devotedly at the edge of the courtyard
Of your solitary life
I will go on drawing the decorative pattern of my songs,
O Unmindful.

EXCHANGE

(*BODOL*)

For nearly two months, from November 7, 1924 to January 3, 1925, Tagore stayed in Argentina and wrote another twenty-six poems. From November 12, he was the guest of Victoria Ocampo, a young writer and emerging literary editor, at her riverside garden house, Miralrio, in San Isidro. He would later dedicate his book of poems *Purabi* to Victoria, whom he named Vijaya.

On the day of Tagore's departure from Buenos Aires on board the *Giulio Cesare*—January 3, 1925—his cabin door had to be taken apart from its hinges so that Vijaya could give him his favourite armchair as a token of her love. He wrote to her on January 5: 'I pass most part of my day and a great part of my night deeply buried in your armchair which, at last, has explained to me the lyrical meaning of the poem of Baudelaire that I read with you.' (Tagore was probably feeling a little too comfortable in Vijaya's armchair!) He wrote only four poems during the eighteen-day voyage from Buenos Aires to Genoa. But the last of this quartet—'Exchange' ('Bodol'), set to music—is especially poignant. The richest gift carries within it the inevitability of loss.

She had a garland in her hand
Made of flowers of smiles
Coloured in so many colours;
I had a burden of fruits of sorrows

Full of the juice of tears.
All of a sudden the damsel came,
Come, she said, and let us exchange.
I looked at her face,
O what a merciless winsome beauty she was!
She took my basket of the wettest rains
And winked with an amused glance,
I took her garland of the newest Spring
And put it close to my heart.
I've won, going along, she said
And smiled and hurried away.
In the evening at the end of the warmest day
*I saw, alas, all the flowers had withered.**

*Trans. by Charu C. Chowdhuri in Rabindranath Tagore, *Purabi: The East in its Feminine Gender*. Trans. by Charu C. Chowdhuri, ed. and intro. by Krishna Bose and Sugata Bose. (London, New York, Calcutta: Seagull Books, 2007), p. 107.

A MADMAN WANDERS

(*SHE KON PAGAL*)

In 1926, Tagore travelled once more to Europe. He went to Italy, Switzerland, Austria, France, England, Norway, Sweden, Denmark, and then back towards Central Europe. He wrote the next song on the night of September 8, 1926 in his railway compartment as his train crossed the Baltic Sea between Copenhagen and Hamburg. Prashanta Chandra Mahalanobis and his wife Nirmalkumari were among his travelling companions. He taught Nirmalkumari Mahalanobis the tune in case he himself forgot it.

A madman wanders by your path alone in the night—
Don't call him, don't call him into your yard.
The words he speaks are from a distant land, alas, who can understand,
The tune he plays on his one-stringed lute.
He will be gone, gone before dawn,
Why spread a seat for him in vain.
At the great festival of breaking bonds
He must sing his song in praise of the new light.

WHOSE GLANCE?

(*KAR CHOEKHER CHAOAR*)

On reaching Hamburg, Tagore checked into Hotel Atlantique. He gave a lecture in this north German port city on 'Culture and Progress'. In the midst of his hectic travels, on September 9 and 10, 1926, Tagore wrote two songs. These could have been composed on the banks of the river Padma in East Bengal or in the rural setting of his university at Santiniketan. There is no hint of any foreign influence in these two compositions:

Whose glance comes like a breeze to sway your heart,
That is why you seem strange at all times.
Your smile droops with the burden of tears,
Your thoughts are touched by silence,
Your speech shrouded in a veil of melodies.
The play of some touchstone in your life,
Assembles golden clouds on the expanse of your heart.
The moments along the stream of time
Raise ripples with golden flashes,
In darkness and in light the corner of your eye quivers.

THE ONE WHO REMAINS DESTITUTE

(ROY JE KANGAL)

The one who remains destitute, empty-handed, at day's end
Appears in the depth of the night adorned in dreams.
In light the one who is pale-faced and silent
What radiance his eyes emit in darkness—
Who attaches a welcoming garland to his hair.
The day's weak-stringed veena with its notes of disdain
Resounds with music by night.
The vast song of the sleepless darkness
Rumbles across the sky at whose call—
Who looks on with winkless eyes in the light of the stars.

THE FLUTE OF FREEDOM

(CHHUTIR BANSHI BAJLO)

From Hamburg, Tagore went to Berlin. There he had a meeting with the then German president von Hindenburg. He lectured on Indian philosophy to a packed hall at the Berlin Philharmonic. Tagore sensed that the mood in Germany had changed since his last visit in 1921. On that occasion Tagore had encountered a war-weary, humiliated Germany. In 1926, he noticed a new assertiveness that tended to interpret a message of peace from the East as a sign of weakness. From Berlin, Tagore travelled south to the Bavarian city of Munich. There in just two days he composed four songs of which three tunes have survived.

The flute of freedom sounds there in the blue sky,
Why do I sit alone in my lonely nook.
The shiuli will bloom breaking all bonds,
The buds are swinging across the garden,
The woods are touched by a breeze washed with dew,
I search for a melody in my own mind staring into infinity.
What web of dreams gets woven along the forest path,
That is where light and shade make their acquaintance.

The breath of aroma of the fallen malati
Spreads its tearful mood on the blades of grass,
The sky smiles at the swaying white-tipped reeds—
I search for a melody in my own mind staring into infinity.

WHO IS AWAKE INSIDE YOU?

(TOR BHITARE JAGIA)

Who is awake inside you?
You have kept him firmly bound.
Alas, he craves for light
And chokes with tears.
If the breeze carries the breath of life,
Why does the veena not break into music,
If the heavens gleam with light,
Why are the eyes sunk in darkness?
The message of a new dawn
The birds have spread across the woods,
The hope of a new life
Finds expression in flowers of myriad colours.
There the night has ended,
Here the midnight lamp burns,
Why is your mansion, your universe
Split so in equal measures.

HAVE NO FEAR

(*NAI NAI BHOY*)

Have no fear, victory will come, this door will open,
I know your ties of bondage will break again and again.
Every now and then losing yourself you spend dormant nights,
Again and again you must wrest back your right to this world.
On land and water you have a call, a call to human society,
You will always sing songs in joy and grief, shame and fear.
Blossoming flowers, cascading rivers, will sing to your melodies,
Light and darkness will throb to your rhythms.

MY EMANCIPATION

(*AMAAR MUKTI ALOY ALOY*)

From Munich, Tagore went to Nuremberg. The poet lectured there and on September 19, 1926, composed what was to become one of his best-known songs celebrating the spirit of freedom.

My emancipation is in the effulgence of this sky,
My freedom in the specks of dust, the blades of grass.
On the distant margins of body and mind I lose myself,
My liberation floats high on the melodies of songs.
My freedom is in the centre of everyone's affection,
In the challenging missions that defy grief and danger.
In the fiery heat of the sacrificial arena of the earth's Sustainer,
May I offer my life as oblation in freedom's quest.

IN THE MORNING LIGHT

(*SAKAAL BELAR ALOY BAJE*)

During the autumn of 1926, Tagore travelled extensively in Central Europe. He visited Germany, Czechoslovakia, Austria, and Hungary. On September 19 in Nuremberg, the poet celebrated the spirit of freedom with his song 'Amaar Mukti Aloy Aloyei Akashe' ('My Emancipation is in the Effulgence of the Sky'). On September 20, he composed this song:

In the morning light sounds the bhairavi of the twinge of farewell,
Bring your flute, come poet.
With the shiver of dew on this autumn dawn and the aroma of shiuli flowers
Leave your song in the distraught breeze, if you cannot stay.
Such a sunrise will come again in gold on the radiant horizon,
A white jasmine eardrop sprayed with vermilion.
In the shadow of the plaintive cooing of pigeons, in a dark, tender charming
*   illusion*
Resounding to the anklets jingling to your song
This glow will rise again.

O BELOVED, YOU ARE ENDLESS

(*MADHUR TOMAR SHESH JE NA PAI*)

Tagore next travelled to Stuttgart. Nirmalkumari Mahalanobis tells us in her memoirs that on the afternoon of September 21, he visited a German family and was taken to the terrace of their house for a good view of the city. The crimson rays of the setting sun added a dash of colour to the poet's white hair. On returning to the hotel, Rabindranath wrote: 'Bhalo lagaar shesh je na pai'. Later by changing a few words the song took its current form, addressing the Omnipresent by the appellation 'Madhur'.

O Beloved, you are endless at the end of time—
Your joy pervades the entire universe.
In this corner of the day's end, in the last gold of the evening cloud
My heart is humming towards a destination unknown.
On the aroma-filled breeze of tired flowers at eventide
A formless embrace engulfs my entire being.
At this dust-coloured sunset on the frontiers of this green earth
I hear across forests the lingering note of your infinite song.

THE STREAM OF GRACE

(*CHAHIYA DEKHO RASER SROTE*)

From Stuttgart, Tagore went to Cologne. There, on September 24, 1926, he composed two songs: 'The Stream of Grace' and 'A Drop of Gold at Dawn'.

Look, look at the play of colour on the stream of grace.
Don't, don't try to draw it close to you.
What you wish to keep, and bind to you,
Vanishes into the darkness again and again,
What plays on the strings of the heart's veena
That is just a song, just words.
You cannot touch it, nor has it any measure,
The nectar that is drunk in the assembly of gods.
On the river's flow, in flower-filled forests,
The sweet smile in the corners of one's eyes,
Drink that nectar in solitude,
Accept it as free.

A DROP OF GOLD AT DAWN

(*TUMI USHAR SONAR BINDU*)

On this trip Tagore's companions included his son Rathindranath, daughter-in-law Pratima Debi, and their adopted daughter Nandini, who was just four years old. Nirmalkumari Mahalanobis records that the next delightful song was affectionately addressed to little Nandini.

You are a drop of gold at dawn on the ocean shore of my heart,
The first dew of an autumn morning on the first shiuli flower.
Indra's bow across the sky leaning towards the ground,
The daughter of paradise bathed in the moon's lustre,
The dream of the crescent moon touched by white clouds,
The secret of the celestial world divulged on this earth.
You are the picture of the poet's meditation, a memory from a previous life,
You are my long-lost song rediscovered by chance.
The words that cannot be spoken except in hushed tones,
You are my freedom come in the form of bondage,
Opening the door, you have called me to the pure light of the lotus grove.

IN SONGS LET YOUR BONDS BE BROKEN

(*GAANE GAANE TABA BONDHAN*)

The following day, September 25, 1926, Tagore was in Dusseldorf. There he composed 'In songs let your bonds be broken'. In the midst of lectures, meetings, and hectic sightseeing the poet's quest for freedom was expressed in this song:

In songs let your bonds be broken
Raising a lament in the darkness of the stifled voice.
Where the veena of the universe plays in the global poet's heart
Let life tumble down there with the flow of your melody.
A break in your rhythm creates conflict in the heart,
The inner and outer selves cannot sing in harmony.
A tuneless heart is a terrible obstacle—it is a blinding storm, an enigma,
Forgetful singer, take back your song, let that hazard be gone.

WHERE AM I WITHIN ME?

(APNI AMAAR KONKHANE)

After seeing his son Rathindranath who was recovering from a surgery in Berlin, Tagore went to Dresden to give a lecture and watch the play *Dakghar* (*Post Office*). Ramananda Chattopadhyay has left vivid descriptions of the crowd that thronged Tagore's lecture as well as the enactment of *Dakghar*. Upon returning to Berlin on October 6, Tagore composed 'Where am I within me?' in search of his own identity.

Where am I within me?
I roam around in that search.
The one who travels in different forms and garbs in the land of shadows
What in the end will his identity be after tears and laughter, who knows.
The one whose voice I heard in the depth of my songs
I cannot find his abode.
The day draws to a close, the light grows faint—
What does the wayside flute say in the afternoon melody.

O BEAUTIFUL

(OGO SUNDAR, EKADA KI JANI)

On October 9, 1926, Tagore left Berlin for Prague, the capital of Czechoslovakia, where he stayed for five days. His old friends, Professor Winternitz and Professor Lesny, had organized a lecture by him. One day they went to a Bach concert where a poet-musician named Zemlinsky sang one of Tagore's songs in Czech. In Prague, too, Tagore watched performances of his play *Dakghar* (Post Office) in German and Czech. During his stay in Prague on October 11 and 12, Rabindranath composed two songs. The first of these was the delectable 'O Beautiful' in the Desh raga.

Once, I wonder in reward for what virtue, O Beautiful,
I, a wild flower, found a place on the garland round your neck.
The first young light at dawn then
Had enchanted the earth's freshly awakened eyes,
Morning melodies played on the veena of youth on water and on land.
Now at the waning of this weary day
In fading light, when the birds' songs are languid,
If at last withered with fatigue this flower drops to earth,
Let the evening wind beyond the darkness
Sweep it along following your footsteps,
Let it not be scattered and tattered in the dust by the careless moments.

IN SEARCH OF THE ULTIMATE END

(*KOTHAY PHIRISH PARAM SHESHER ANWESHWANE*)

Where do you roam in search of the ultimate end,
He is here endless in this universe.
His words come with both hands outstretched in a child's guise,
Calls you babbling close to your breast,
His touch can be felt in that forest of flowers.
Where do you roam in search of your own?
He appears as a stranger at every moment.
His abode is at the outside door of every home,
His light is by the side of every path,
His figure is in secret form in every heart.

YOU HAVE FREEDOM IN THE SKY

(*AKASHE TOR TEMNI AACHHE CHHUTI*)

Tagore's next destination was Austria's capital Vienna where sober expressions of bourgeois high culture mingled with the youthful avant-garde. On October 16, 1926, Tagore delivered a lecture. But then his health suffered and doctors ordered him ten days of complete rest. However, that did not stop him from composing a song. On October 20, he wrote 'You Have Freedom in the Sky'.

You have freedom in the sky,
Let your two wings not remain unused.
O bird, deep inside the woods
The nest makes you forget with its deception,
The night lies to you,
It will never loosen its grip.
Don't you know in what hope
You break out in song in your slumber.
Don't you know in the midst of the darkness at dawn
Light's hope sings its deep melody,
Light's hope does not remain hidden,
It breaks the bond of the closed bud.

I HAVE NOT REACHED THE END OF THE ROAD

(PATH EKHONO SHESH HOLO NA)

Before he had fully recovered, Tagore set out on the road again. On October 26, 1926, he reached Budapest, the capital of Hungary, and gave a lecture there. Despite being in bad health, Tagore composed a song on October 27. Nirmalkumari Mahalanobis remembered: 'Soon after reaching Budapest, the first song was written—"Path Ekhono Shesh Holo Na". That languid evening, the white snow covering the terraces and trees all around had created a realm of enchantment. The bone-weary poet sat down on a big chair in the living room and wrote this song:

I have not reached the end of the road, the brilliance of the day is fading.
Between you and me, alas, the darkness of night will descend.
Now bring your flame
And light my lamp,
We will be united in the lustre, travelling companions on the road.
I cannot see your face clearly, O Beautiful—
That is why the terrible weariness of the long journey entwines me.
Turning in the shadows, moving in the dust,
I cannot express my deepest thoughts,
The last word will now be lit up by your lamp and mine.

YOUR FLUTE

(*DINER BELAY BANSHI TOMAR BAJIECHHILE*)

During the autumn of 1926, Tagore visited Germany, Czechoslovakia, Austria, and Hungary. After his arrival in Hungary, he fell seriously ill. On his doctors' advice, he spent a few days at a health resort on the banks of Balaton Lake. He composed a song during his stay at Balaton— 'Pantho-Pakhir Rikta Kulay Boner Gopan Dale' ('In the Empty Home of the Travelling Bird on the Secret Forest Branch')—but its tune has been lost. The day before coming to Balaton, on October 30, 1926 in Budapest, he wrote this song:

During the day you had played your flute in many tunes,
Your song's touch reached my heart, you yourself remained distant.
As I ask the wayfarers 'Who played this flute',
They beguile me with various names, I roam around at different doors.
Now the sky turns pale, the tired day shuts its eyes,
If you make me wander along different paths, I shall die of a fruitless search.
From the outside come inside and spread your own mat,
Come and play your flute
In the inner quarters of my heart.

O FORMLESS

(ARUP, TOMAR BANI)

At his hotel in Balaton, Prashanta Chandra Mahalanobis encouraged Tagore to adopt a new German technique of writing on an aluminium plate with a special ink and printing directly from it. Tagore's book *Lekhan* was published using this technique. On November 8, 1926, Tagore planted a tree on the lakeshore. He wrote: 'When I am no longer on the earth, my tree, let the ever-renewed leaves of thy spring murmur to the wayfarers: "The poet did love while he lived."' On November 12, he left Budapest on a lecture tour that took him to Zagreb, Belgrade, Sofia, and Bucharest. Here in the capital of Romania he gave final shape to his song 'O Formless', which he had originally drafted in Zagreb on November 13.

O Formless, let your message
Bring freedom to my body, to my mind.
Your eternal festival is the world's illumination—
I am just its earthen lamp, light its flame
Inextinguishable, luminous, your wish.
Just as your spring breeze writes lyrics of songs
In colours, flowers, leaves and woods in all directions

Blow the breath of life into the inner recesses of my heart,
Let its emptiness filled to the brim be blessed with tunes—
Its misfortune purified by your auspicious hand.

HAVE I NOT PLAYED THE FLUTE?

(BANSHI AMI BAJAINI KI)

Tagore boarded a ship from the Romanian Black Sea port of Constanza and sailed to Istanbul in Turkey and on to Piraeus in Greece. From Piraeus, he travelled by car to Athens. On the way back from Athens to Piraeus, he wrote this song:

Have I not played the flute by the wayside?
Have I not finished rendering my songs at your outside door?
There is the door's curtain designed in many colours and pictures
I have laid offerings of various melodies there again and again.
Today I seem to hear a final message on water and on land—
'Free yourself of the bondage of the road'—it says.
The endless oscillation between separation touched with union
Finish it and take me beyond these comings and goings.

ALL THE WOUNDS, AS MANY LOSSES

(*KSHATA JATO, KSHATI JATO*)

On November 25, 1926, in Piraeus he wrote, 'All the Wounds, as Many Losses'. This European trip had begun with a visit to Italy. Some of his statements, interpreted not entirely fairly as admiration for Mussolini's fascist regime, had attracted criticism. Tagore felt hurt, and seems to be transcending his sense of being wronged in this song:

All the wounds, as many losses, more false than falsehoods,
The moment's young, sharp blades of grass will remain below.
What did not happen, what you did not get, who has not repaid your debt,
That is all a mirage, and will vanish behind you.
This image of incomparable beauty your eyes have just seen
The morning sun on the crimson horizon—
This is the ultimate gift, the fulfilment of life,
Truth's joyous manifestation
Here it rises.

WHAT I RECEIVED ON THE FIRST DAY

(*JA PEYECHHI PRATHAM DINE*)

On the same day, he composed another song affirming his deep faith:

What I received on the first day, may I receive in the end,
Touch the world with two hands laughing like a child.
At the moment of departure with ease
May I complete my obeisance,
May I stand where all the paths converge.
Let my eyes witness the One for whom no search is needed,
Let me feel the touch of the One who always remains near.
The One in whose lap I ever reside—
Let me tell Him as I leave—
I am blessed in this life loving you.

THE PLAINTIVE FLUTE ON A FOREIGN BOAT

(*SAKARUNA BENU BAJAYE KE JAY BIDESHI NAYE*)

It was as an intellectual pilgrim that in July 1927 the poet travelled east from Madras on the French ship *Amboise*. 'India's learning had once spread outside India,' Tagore wrote, '[b]ut the people outside accepted it ... We have embarked on this pilgrimage to see the signs of the history of India's entry into the universal.' The *Amboise* arrived at Singapore on July 20, 1927. After spending more than three weeks in the Malayan peninsula, the poet travelled to Indonesia. As he journeyed from Singapore across the straits of Malacca towards Batavia, he wrote his poem 'Srivijayalakshmi' celebrating the renewal of a bond between Bengal and Srivijaya after a thousand-year separation. After visiting Java and Bali, Rabindranath wrote one of his most beautiful poems, 'Bali', which was later renamed more generically 'Sagarika' ('Sea Maiden').

On the ship *Maier* travelling from Java to Singapore, on October 2, 1927, Tagore wrote what was to become one of his most popular songs.

Who goes playing that plaintive flute on a foreign boat?
I can feel the touch of that melody.
The unknown anguish of whose faraway forlorn heart

Comes floating riding that tune on the ocean shore's restless breeze
In the shadow of the woods.
Listening to it today in my solitary foreign abode
Bhairavi wet with autumn dew sounds silently in the depth of my heart.
An image comes to mind in light and song—as if on the desolate river path
Who goes to the water to fill her pitcher with languid footsteps
In the shadow of the woods.

SWINGING IN THE WOODS

(*SHE DIN DUJANE*)

On October 5, 1927, Tagore left Penang by train and reached Bangkok, the capital of Thailand, on October 8. His poem 'Siam' composed on October 11, 1927, gave poetic expression to Tagore's search for a greater India.

On October 15, he left Bangkok on the return journey to Penang. He wrote this song on the train:

That day we two had swung in the woods, the swing tied with a string of
*   flowers.*
Let that bit of memory sometimes flicker in your mind, do not forget.
In the breeze that day, you know, had mingled my mind's delirium,
Across the sky there was spread the likeness of your smile.
As we went along the path on that full moon night, the moon had risen in
*   the sky,*
You and I had met who knows at what a great auspicious moment.
Now my time is gone, I will bear alone the burden of parting—
The thread of love I strung around your heart, do not untie it, do not.

A FIERCE GUST OF WIND

(*KHARA BAYU BOY BEGE*)

In Penang on October 18, 1927, two days before his voyage back to India, Tagore composed this beautiful song as he witnessed another tropical storm gathering on the horizon:

A fierce gust of wind , the clouds envelop all directions,
O boatman, row your boat.
Hold the helm in your tight grasp, I will lift and tie the sail—
Come, pull with force, heave-ho.
The chains clank and clatter again and again, this is not the boat's fearful
*   cry—*
The tether of restraint is not tolerable any more, that is why today it is reeling.
Come, pull with force, heave-ho.
Counting the days and moments do not agitate your mind
Do not say 'to go or not to go'.
The ocean of doubt you will cross within,
Do not look outside in anxiety.
If the Destroyer dances, his wild matted locks storm-ravaged, the waves
*   billow,*
Do not be diffident, dance to his rhythm—sing the song of victory.
Come, pull with force, heave-ho.

GLORY TO YOU

(*NAMO NAMO SHACHICHITARANJANA*)

Tagore travelled to Europe and the United States in 1930 and to Iran and Iraq in 1932. These voyages yielded a rich harvest of travel literature, poems, paintings, and poem-paintings, but no songs. Tagore's universalist sentiment was perhaps best expressed in a poem-painting signed 'Baghdad May 24 1932' at the end of the visit to Iran and Iraq.

Abasan holo rati
Nibaiya phelo kalima-molin
Gharer koner bati.
Nikhiler alo purba akashe
Jwalilo punyadine
Eksathe jara chalibe tahara
Sakalere nik chine.

The night has ended.
Put out the light of the lamp
of thine own narrow corner
smudged with smoke.
The great morning which is for all
*   appears in the East.*

49

Let its light reveal us
to each other
who walk on
the same
>   *path of pilgrimage.*

In May 1934, Tagore embarked on his final voyage outside India to nearby Sri Lanka. After spending a week from May 11 to 18 in Colombo, Tagore arrived in Panadura. There by the ocean shore Rabindranath composed a new song for his drama *Shapmochan*—a song extraordinarily rich in its allusions to ancient Indian mythology.

Glory to you, king of gods, dispeller of sorrows,
Graceful as the monsoon cloud, with deep blue eyes, glory to you.
In the shadow of the avenue of paradise, at your footfall from the new
>   *divine tree*
Floats a waft of fragrance on a romantic night—glory to you.
To the rhythm of your sidelong glance Menoka's string of jingling anklets
Awakens to music, sweeter than the humming of bees—glory to you.

SONGS IN FIVE
GENRES

PREM (LOVE)

YOUR VEENA HAD SONGS

(*TOMAR BINAY GAAN CHHILO*)

Your veena had songs, and my basket had flowers.
We two swayed that day in the same southern breeze.
That day no one knows what waves filled the sky,
Your boat of melodies came ashore near my colourful flowers.
That day I felt, to the rhythm of your songs
Flowers will bloom in my heart forever.
Yet the songs floated away, the flowers finished at day's end,
In the sweet play of springtime, somewhere, alas, there was a mistake.

ARE YOU ONLY AN IMAGE?

(*TUMI KI KEBOLI CHHABI*)

This song, part of a longer poem, was inspired by the memory of a particular woman, the poet's sister-in-law Kadambari Debi, who took her own life in 1884. No woman ever touched Tagore so deeply and the poet never ceased to anguish over her loss. Kadambari Debi's haunting presence can be felt in some of Rabindranath's finest poems, songs, stories, and paintings. 'Chhabi' was composed soon after the poet chanced upon a picture of his lost beloved in October 1914 during a stay in Allahabad. The English translation is by my maternal grandfather Charu Chandra Chowdhuri.

Are you only an image, only on canvas
    Painted?
Those far-off nebulae
That crowd into their nest in the sky,
Those pilgrims unto the dark,
Journeying day and night, with torches
    of light,
The planets, the stars, the sun,
Are you not as real as they are?

An image only are you?
You are not before my eyes,
It is within their depth that you live.
And so, today you are the green of the
    green earth,
And the blue of the blue sky
And in you my world has found its heart's desire.
I do not know and nobody knows,
It is your music that I sing in my songs
And it is you who is the poet in the poet's mind.
Not a likeness, not a painting,
Not a mere image are you.

I KNOW YOU

(AMI CHINI GO CHINI TOMARE)

I know you, I do know you, O Bideshini,*
You live beyond the ocean, O Bideshini.
I have seen you on autumn mornings, I have seen you on honeyed nights,
I have seen you in the depths of my heart, O Bideshini.
I have tuned my ear to the sound of the heavens and heard your song,
I have devoted my life to you, O Bideshini.
After roaming the entire universe I have come to a new land,
I am a guest at your door, O Bideshini.

---

*This song is addressed to bideshini, literally, woman from another land, but in the depths of its meaning truly untranslatable.

DID YOU NOT RECOGNIZE ME?

(CHINILE NA AMARE KI)

Did you not recognize me!
In a lantern-less corner, unmindful I was there, you turned away seeing
*   no one.*
Having come to the door you forgot it would have opened at your touch—
The boat of my destiny dashed against this tiny obstacle.
During the stormy night I was counting the moments.
Alas, I did not hear, I did not hear, the chariot's sound, your chariot's sound.
Trembling at the roar of thunder I had clasped my breast,
The flash of lightning wrote my doom across the sky.

O LISTEN, WHO PLAYS THAT MUSIC?

(*OGO SHONO KE BAJAY*)

O listen, who plays that music?
The fragrance of the garland of forest flowers blends with the flute's melody.
Touching the lower lip the flute steals that smile,
My beloved's smile floats with the honeyed song towards my heart.
The bumblebee of the forest bower seems to hum inside the flute,
The distraught bakul flowers blossom with the flute's tune.
Jamuna's rippling melody reaches my ears, my heart weeps,
At who does that sweet moon in the sky gaze and smile.

YOUR LETTER HAS TURNED TO DUST

(LIKHAN TOMAR DHULAY HOYECHHE DHULI)

Your letter has turned to dust in the dust,
The characters of your alphabet have been lost.
I sit alone on a spring night, do I see again,
The lines drawn by your playful pen in the forest?
Have your old letters arrived by some error in the new leaves?
So many mallikas in the gardens today
Bloom like your aroma-filled name.
The message touched by your soft fingers reminds me today
Of which script of separation filled with pain.
On the madhabi bough rises and swings your letters of old.

THE POLE STAR OF MY LIFE

(TOMAREI KORIACHHI JIBANER DHRUBATARA)

I have made you the Pole Star of my life,
In this ocean I will not lose my way again.
Wherever I travel you stay luminous,
Shining rays of mercy on my tears of distress.
Your face ever rises secretly in my mind,
A moment's delay makes me lose my bearings.
If ever my heart is tempted to go astray
A glimpse of your face shames it to correct course.

IN THIS DARK SOLITARY ROOM

(*SAKHI AANDHAARE EKELA*)

Friend, in this dark solitary room my heart is restless.
Pursuing which desire, where will it go, the path is unknown.
In a watery torrent, in dense darkness, in the tear-laden breeze
Whose message ever wafts to my ears and ever does not.

YOUR INTIMATION

(*HE SOKHA BAROTA PEYECHHI*)

O beloved, my heart has received your intimation from your breath's touch,
Unseen friend, you have come on the southern breeze.
Why do you deny me, why tie me in invisible threads
Reveal yourself, reveal yourself fully in body and mind in my arbour.
Reveal yourself in magnolias, in flowers rich in red and gold.
Why do you just tempt me far away with your flute's melody?
In the festival of youth let me nab you within the bond of beholding.

WHO JUST WAFTED ACROSS MY HEART

(*AMAAR PRANER PORE CHOLE GELO*)

*Who just wafted across my heart
Like the gentle spring breeze?
Touching and bowing down as she went—
She made hundreds of flowers bloom.
She has gone, leaving not a word, where did she go never to return.
Going away she cast a glance, what was it that she sang?
That is why I wait alone in this thicket of flowers.
Like a wave she has drifted away, gone to the land of moonbeams,
Where she passed smiling, there she has left her smile,
Perhaps beckoning me, I feel, from the corner of her eyes.
Where will I go, where, I wonder sitting alone.
She has caressed the moon's eyes with the spell of sleep.
She has swung a string of flowers somewhere in my heart.
Whatever she said as she crossed the flower-thicket,
The flowers' aroma going wild departed with her.
My heart aches, my eyelids droop,
Which way, where did she go?*

THROUGH YOUR EYES

(*OGO TOMAR CHOKKHU DIYE*)

O, through your eyes I can see truth
You are the first to create my true form.
I bow to you, I bow to you,
I bow to you a hundred times.
I am the young ray of the morning sun,
I am an unblemished streak of light,
I am the first shower of mercy
Of the fresh dark clouds.
I bow to you, I bow to you,
I bow to you a hundred times.

THAT I COULD NOT FORGIVE HER

(*KHOMITE PARILAM NA*)

That I could not forgive her
Forgive my wretchedness, O Lord, the refuge of all sinners!
It dies of agony, it dies of shame, love's frailty.
Forgive my wretchedness, O Lord, the refuge of all sinners!
I could not clasp my beloved to my breast, love have I destroyed,
In seeking to punish the sinner I have invited sin.
I know you will forgive her
The luckless one, bowed at your feet burdened by sin.
You will not forgive, forgive not
My lack of forgiveness, O Lord, the refuge of all sinners!

PUJA (DEVOTION)

❧

MY BOAT LADEN WITH SONGS

(KUL THEKE MOR GAANER TARI)

I am untethering my boat laden with songs from the shore,
Setting it afloat mid-ocean, its sail fluttering.
Where the cuckoo calls under the shadow, not there,
Where the village bride goes to fetch water, not there,
Where the blue play of death rises and billows,
There I am setting my boat full of songs free.
Now, veena, you and I, we are alone—
Who cares we cannot see anyone in the darkness.
The flower that is plucked from a forest bower, not that flower,
The flower that swings from a window creeper, not that flower,
The boundless, sky-filled flowers of melodies
I am untethering my boat laden with songs in that direction.

❧

HARMONY WITH YOUR TUNES

(*AMAAR BELA JE JAY*)

My time passes in the evening hours
Seeking harmony with your tunes.
My lute with its single string
Cannot carry the strains of the songs,
With you again and again
I have lost in this play
Seeking harmony with your tunes.
This string is tuned to a melody that is near,
That flute sounds in the distance.
At that shore of your play of songs
Can everyone join
Across the ocean of the heart of the universe
In the webs cast by melodies
Seeking harmony with your tunes?

THE RUSTLING SOUND

(AJI MARMARDHWANI KENO JAGILO RE)

Why has the rustling sound arisen today?
In my buds and blossoms, in swaying waves
I can feel a trembling shiver.
Which beggar, alas, has come to my courtyard's door,
Appearing to claim all I possess.
My heart seems to know him,
Sprouting flowers to his songs.
Today that traveller's footsteps sound in the depth of my heart,
That is why, startled, I wake up from my sleep.

ALL THE SONGS THAT I SANG FOR YOU

(AMI TOMAY JATO SHUNIECHHILEM GAAN)

All the songs that I sang for you—
I do not seek any gift in return.
If you forget those songs, you may forget
When the stars rise in the evening on the ocean shore,
When I conclude at your assembly
A few of my melodies of this brief sojourn.
Your countless songs that you sang for me
How can you forget that memory?
That truth, poet, you will remember
On rain-resonant nights, in the spring breeze—
It is just this that leaves a sense of hurt
Can you forget that you stole my heart?

YOU HAVE MADE ME ENDLESS

(*AMARE TUMI ASHESH KORECHHO*)

You have made me endless, such is your grace,
Emptied and filled me again, with life ever new.
Across so many hills, along so many riverbanks
Have you roamed bearing this little flute,
So many tunes have you played again and again
Who should I tell of it.
At that immortal touch of yours my overflowing heart
Lost in a profound limitless joy, finds utterance.
Filling just one cup of my hands
You are pouring your gifts day and night,
So many ages pass and you are not done
I remain your receptacle.

I GLIMPSE YOU NOW AND THEN

(MAJHE MAJHE TABA DEKHA PAI)

I glimpse you now and then, why can I not see you forever?
Why do clouds gather on my heart's horizon, hiding you from my sight?
In fleeting light when I see you in the twinkling of an eye
Ever haunted by the fear of losing you, I lose you in an instant.
Tell me what must I do to find you, and keep you in my vision?
Where can I find so much love, O Lord, to entwine you to my heart?
I will not look at another again, I will make this solemn promise,
If you say so, I will banish at once all worldly desires.

WHY SHOULD YOU KEEP ME
IN COMFORT?

(*SUKHE AMAY RAKHBE KENO*)

Why should you keep me in comfort, hold me in your bosom?
   Let contentment burn to ash.
Let the ground under my feet be gone, you will then hold me tight,
Pick me up and swing me to the rhythm of your arms.
Let the flood come if it will where I set up my home,
If you sweep me away I do not wish to be saved.
Accepting defeat, I have lost my fear—your victory is mine as well
I will surrender, for that is how I will capture you for myself.

GAZING AT THIS PATH

(*AMAAR EI PATH CHAOATEI ANANDA*)

My bliss is in gazing at this path.
Sun and clouds play, rains come, and spring.
Who are they before me coming and going with news,
I remain happy in solitary contemplation—a gentle breeze blows.
All day long, eyes wide open, I will be at the door alone.
When the auspicious moment comes suddenly I will catch my glimpse.
Until then, every moment, I laugh and sing in my own mind,
Until then, in anticipation floats in a beautiful aroma.

UNITE ME

(OTHER SATHE MILAO)

Unite me with those who graze your cows,
Those who play the flute in your name.
At the quay paved with stone in this bustle of the mart
What enticement has brought me here?
What calls do the forest leaves bring, whose beckoning the blades of grass!
My beloved in a playful mood plays in the playroom of my heart,
That is the message the birds' calls have brought.

ON THE OTHER SHORE OF MY SONGS

(*DANRIYE AACHHO TUMI AMAAR GAANER OPAARE*)

You stand there on the other shore of my songs,
My tunes find their verse at your feet, I cannot reach you.
The agitated wind blows, do not keep your boat tethered any more,
Come, come, cross over to the core of my heart.
My play of songs with you is a play from afar,
The pain of separation finds its melody in the flute all day.
When will you take my flute and come and play it yourself
In the dense darkness of the joyful silent night?

THE UNIVERSE THROUGH SONGS

(*GAANER BHITOR DIYE JAKHAN DEKHI*)

When I see the universe through songs,
Then do I recognize, then do I know it.
Then in the language of its light the sky fills with love,
Then a message sublime rises from its specks of dust.
It is then that from the outside it enters within me,
Then my heart shivers with the blades of grass.
The frontiers of beauty in the flow of grace transcend their own limits,
Then I see I am in whispering intimacy with all.

BOW MY HEAD

(AMAAR MATHA NATO KORE DAO)

Bow my head below the dust of your feet.
Drown all of my pride in the tears of my eyes.
In craving self-glory, I only humiliate myself,
By circling around my Self I die every moment.
Drown all of my pride in the tears of my eyes.
May I not aggrandize myself in my own work,
May your wishes find fulfilment in the midst of my life.
I yearn for your ultimate peace, your supreme splendour in my heart,
Protect me by taking your place in the lotus-petal of my heart
Drown all of my pride in the tears of my eyes.

I WILL SING FOR YOU

(TOMAY GAAN SHONABO)

I will sing for you, that is why you keep me awake
O dispeller of sleep.
That is why you startle my heart with your call
O rouser of sorrow.
Darkness descends, birds return to their nests,
Boats come ashore,
Only my heart finds no rest
O rouser of sorrow.
In the midst of my work
You do not let the pendulum of tears and laughter stop.
Having touched me and filled my life with nectar
You move away,
Perhaps you wait in the shadow of my pain
O rouser of sorrow.

CROSSING THE OCEAN OF DEATH

(AMI MARER SAGAR PARI DEBO)

I will cross the ocean of death riding the fierce stormy wind
In this fear-conquering boat of mine.
Buoyed by the message to fear not, with large-hearted faith in the torn sail
The boat will cross to your shore in the shade of the shadowy trees.
The one who wants me will show me the way,
In fearless mind I will set sail, for that alone I am responsible.
When the day ends, I know, on reaching the harbour
The blood-red lotus of my sad days I will submit at your merciful feet.

ALL MEANNESS IS DEVOURED*

(SARBAKHARBATARE DAHE TABA KRODHADAHA)

All meanness is devoured by the fire of your anger,
O God, give us strength, have mercy on your devotees.
Sweep away, Almighty, what is false and petty,
May death be dwarfed by the ecstasy of life.
By churning the depths of suffering will be found immortality,
Those who fear death will be freed of their terror.
Your resplendent scorching power will melt and let flow
Freed of the chain of stones a stream of sacrifice.

*Composed by Tagore in 1929 on hearing the news of the death of the young political prisoner Jatin Das in Lahore Jail following a two-month hunger strike.

PRAKRITI (NATURE)

THE SKY FILLED WITH THE SUN
AND STARS

(AKASH BHORA SURYA TARA)

The sky filled with the sun and stars, the universe brimming with life,
In the midst of it all I have found my place,
That is why in wonder I break into song.
The surge of infinite time that rocks the world between high tide and low
Pulsates in my veins, in my streams of blood,
That is why in wonder I break into song.
I have stepped on the blades of grass walking along the forest path,
The aroma of flowers has sent a thrill through my heart,
The gifts of joy are outspread,
That is why in wonder I break into song.
Straining my ears, eyes wide open I have poured my heart into the earth's
*   bosom,*
I have searched for the unknown amidst the known,
That is why in wonder I break into song.

THE SPELL OF THE FULL MOON

(PURNO CHANDER MAYAY)

Under the spell of the full moon tonight my thoughts lose their way,
Birds on the ocean shore as if, away, away, away they go.
In a melody of light and shade in the distance of another age
Come, come, come, they call.
Where my lost spring nights have fled
There they search for their own mate again and again.
Where in light and shade what anguish from a remote past
Says in lament, alas, alas, alas.

IN THE DARK SKY

(AANDHAR AMBARE PRACHANDA DAMBARU)

In the dark sky terrible drumbeats
Resound with a deafening roar.
The blossoming trees are in restless sway
Across the wind-swept horizon.
Clamorous rivers, rustling woods,
Waterfalls in torrential overflow,
The sounds pour into the depths of music,
The monsoon ascetic composes melodies.
The intoxicating aroma of kadamba flowers
Are looted in profusion by the wild gusts.
Flashes of lightning unite the skies,
The terrified night lets out a scream,
The dance of a frenzied demon as if
Raiding the gate of the fortress of clouds.

ACROSS MANY AGES

(BOHU JUGER OPAR HOTE)

Across many ages monsoon comes to my mind,
The rhythm of which poet sounds in the steady downpour of rain?
The garlands of union that had mixed with dust into dust
Their fragrance floats in today with the moist breeze.
That day clouds like this had gathered on the banks of the river Reba,
The rain had come down like this on the green mountain ridge.
Malabika had gazed with unblinking eyes at the path,
That wistful look comes floating with the shadow of the dark clouds.

THE DEEP DENSE DELUSION OF SRABAN

(AJI SRABAN GHANAGAHAN MOHE)

Today in the deep dense delusion of Sraban with secret footsteps
Like the night, O silent one, you came avoiding everyone's gaze.
The dawn today has shut its eyes, the breeze comes calling in futility,
Over the shameless blue sky who has spread the thick cover of clouds.
Forestland bereft of birdsong, closed doors at every home—
Who are you, solitary traveller on a deserted road?
O lonely friend, O beloved, my room is open—
Do not pass before me like a dream neglectfully casting me aside.

MY NIGHT ENDS ON AN AUTUMN DAWN

(*AMAAR RAAT POHALO*)

My night ends on an autumn dawn.
Flute, in whose hands will I leave you?
So many tunes have sounded in your breast
Themes of farewells and advents,
In spring and rain on so many dawns and nights.
The message that remains hidden in the heart, invisible,
You had stolen it in music, in song.
The time for it is gone
Like the stars at night's end,
Finish it with the withering of the shiuli flowers.

YOU TOLD ME THE OTHER DAY
(*SEDIN AMAY BOLECHHILE*)

[Translated by Charu C. Chowdhuri]*

You told me the other day
My time has not come yet,
And then you turned away.
It was playtime then,
Mallikas bloomed in the woods,
And all the time an eager wind blew
Among the twigs and leaves.
Winter's day has come today
Shrouded in mist, unadorned.
Daylight fades,
Has not the time come yet?
On the doorstep at the end,
I look forward and wait.

---

*Rabindranath Tagore, *Purabi: The East in its Feminine Gender*, trans. by Charu C. Chowdhuri, edited and introduced by Krishna Bose and Sugata Bose, (London, New York, Kolkata: Seagull Books, 2007), p. 159.

MY HEART GROWS WISTFUL

(*MAMO ANTARA UDASHE*)

My heart grows wistful
The leaves rustle in a restless breeze.
The night bathed in moonlight at the edge of waking and sleep
Is flustered and distraught at the fragrant end of whose sari,
It will not let me stay at home, takes me out where,
Towards what a beautiful faraway heavenly sky,
On the shores of days past, by the side of an ocean of memories
To the anguish hidden in the hint of a lament.

IF I DO NOT RECOGNIZE HIM

(*JADI TARE NAI CHINI GO*)

If I do not recognize him, will he be able to choose me
In this new day of spring—I do not know, I know not.
Will he speak into the ears of my bud in songs?
Stealing its heart on this new day of spring,
I do not know, I know not.
Will he colour the flowers with his own colours?
Will he enter the core of my heart and wake me up?
Will my veil of new leaves swing suddenly at his touch?
Will he win my secret passion on this new day of spring,
I do not know, I know not.

SWADESH (PATRIOTISM)*

MY GOLDEN BENGAL

(AMAAR SONAR BANGLA)

My golden Bengal, I love you.
Ever your sky, ever your breeze, play a flute in my heart.
O Mother, in spring your mango groves spread their maddening aroma,
O Mother, in autumn in your overflowing rice fields what a sweet smile I
*   have seen.*
What lustre and what shade, what affection and what charm,
What a sari's end you have spread under the trees, on the banks of rivers.
Mother, words from your lips pour nectar in my ears,
Mother, if your face looks pale, O Mother, my eyes are filled with tears.
I spent my childhood in this playroom of yours,
By smearing my body with the dust of your earth I feel my life fulfilled.
When day ends and evening comes what lamp do you light in your room,
Leaving off all play then, O Mother, I run into your arms.

---

*Based on and modified from an unpublished translation by Charu C.
Chowdhuri in the collection of Krishna Bose.

In your meadows where the cattle graze, at your ferry ghat to cross the river,
On your shadowy village paths where the birds chirp all day,
In your grain-filled yard where life's story unfolds,
O Mother, all of them, your shepherds, your peasants, are my brothers.
O Mother, I bow my head at your feet—
Give me the dust of your feet, it will be the jewel on my head.
O Mother, I will offer at your feet all of a poor man's riches,
I will not buy at another's shop again, O Mother, an ornament that is a
     noose.

O MY COUNTRY'S SOIL

(O AMAAR DESHER MATI)

O my country's soil, I bow my head to you.
On you is spread the universe-encompassing universal mother's sari's end.
You have blended with my body,
You have united with my mind and soul,
The dark, gentle image of yours is etched in the core of my heart.
O Mother, my birth is in your lap, my death at your breast.
You are the venue of all my play in sorrow and joy.
You have fed me your grain,
You have comforted me with cool water,
You are the all-suffering all-enduring mother's mother.
O Mother, I have drawn so much on you, taken so much, mother,
Yet I do not know what I have given you, mother
My life is wasted in fruitless tasks,
I spend my days within the limits of my room,
You gave me strength to no purpose, O giver of strength!

SHINE ON ALONE

(*JADI TOR DAK SHUNE*)

If no one answers your call, then go on alone.
Go on alone, go on alone, go on alone.
If no one speaks up, O Unfortunate,
If all turn their faces away, everyone is afraid,
Then open your heart
Speak your mind clearly alone.
If all return, O Unfortunate,
If no one looks at you as you venture on the dense path,
Then crush the thorns on the path with your blood-soaked feet alone.
If no one raises a lamp, O Unfortunate,
If on dark stormy nights they shut their doors on you,
Then in the fire of lightning
Lighting up the ribs on your chest, shine on alone.

BRACE YOURSELF

(BUK BENDHE TUI DANRA DEKHI)

Brace yourself and stand, brother, do not bend yet again!
Do not through ceaseless worry spurn the riches you have in hand.
Decide on something, drifting aimlessly is worse than death,
Sometimes this way, sometimes that, do not play this game any more, brother.
Whether or not you find the treasure, you must still care and persevere,
If what you find falls short of expectations, do not shed tears, brother.
If you must set sail on your boat, do not dilly-dally any more,
Do not open your eyes when the moment has passed, brother.

WHOEVER ELSE MAY ABANDON YOU

(*JE TOMAY CHHARE CHHARUK*)

Whoever else may abandon you, I will not leave you, Mother!
I will find refuge at your feet, O Mother, at your feet,
I will not care for anyone else, Mother.
Who says your home is poor, your heart is filled with countless jewels,
I know their worth, I will not crave another's affection, Mother.
Your tattered quilt is spread, I cannot forget that, Mother.
With the pull of riches, honour, popular acclaim, they try to tempt me,
O Mother, fear rises to the head, I will not lose to anyone, Mother!

THE DAWN OF A NEW AGE

(ORE NUTON JUGER BHORE)

At the dawn of a new age
Do not fritter away your time pondering the right time.
What will remain, what will not, what will happen, what will not
O Calculating,
In the midst of this doubt will you mix your worries?
Just as the waterfall traverses down the difficult mountain
Plunge down carefree on the unknown path.
The more obstacles you face your strength will increase,
You will conquer the unknown and make it known to you.
As you move on the drum of victory will sound,
The movement of your legs takes you along the path, do not delay any more.

BORN IN THIS LAND

(*SARTHAK JANAM AMAAR*)

My life is fulfilled being born in this land.
My life is fulfilled, O Mother, having loved you.
I do not know if you possess rich jewels like a queen,
I only know the bliss I feel coming into your shadow.
I know not in which forest the flowers' aroma causes such restlessness,
In which sky the moon rises with such a smile.
On opening my eyes your light was the first to enchant me,
I will gaze at that light before closing my eyes in the end.

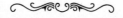

BICHITRA (VARIETY)

FIREFLY

(*JONAKI*)

O firefly, with what cheer have you spread your two wings?
In dim twilight in forest midst, you have poured your heart out in ecstasy.
You are not the sun, not the moon, you are no less joyful for that.
You have fulfilled your life and lit your own flame.
Whatever you have is yours, you are not in debt to anyone,
You have obeyed the dictate of your inner strength.
You transcend the bond of darkness, you are little but not small,
All the lights of the universe you have made your own.

DREAMS IN THE WIND

(*AMI KEBOLI SWAPAN KORECHHI BAPAN*)

I have only sowed dreams in the wind,
That is why I have sought the impossible in despair.
The land disappears like the shadow, the boat of hope cannot find a shore,
An imagined figure floats around in the sky.
Nothing was captured in just a web of desire.
No one was seized by this mere distant quest.
Sitting alone I played with fire in my own mind,
At the end of the day I saw in dismay all had turned to ash.

WHO AMONG YOU WILL CROSS

(OGO TORA KE JABI PARE)

O, who among you will cross.
I am waiting with my boat at the riverbank.
In the grove on the other side
There is so much play among so many,
On this side a desolate arid desert.
There is time yet, who else will come.
Why does time get frittered away thinking many thoughts?
The sun will descend behind the western mountain,
The beautiful breeze will stop,
The ferry will close in the evening darkness.

HIS PLAY THRONE

(KHELAGHAR BANDHTE LEGECHHI)

I am building a house of sand deep in my mind.
So I have stayed awake so many nights, what can I tell you?
At dawn the traveller calls, alas, I can find no rest,
He calls me to the play outside, how can I go?
Scattered about in disdain by others is what is mine
With clods of earth from old broken days I build my house.
The one who is my new playmate, this is his play throne,
The broken he will put together with what mantra!

I ALONE AM LEFT BEHIND

(*AMII SHUDHU ROINU BAKI*)

I alone am left behind.
What was there is gone, what remains is a mere illusion.
Those who were said to be mine, they do not answer my call any more,
Where are they, where are they? I cry out in lament.
Tell me, mother, I ask you—did you keep nothing for me,
How can I live this life only with myself?

IF THE DAY PASSES LIKE THIS

(EMNI KORE JAY JADI DIN)

If the day passes like this, let it.
My mind flies, let it fly spreading wings of songs.
Today tunes rush from the fountain of my heart,
The bonds of this body have broken,
Above my head has opened the blue cover of the sky.
The earth today has spread out its heart,
Whose message is that?
Today the hard soil does not obstruct the mind.
Crafted in what melody
The universe utters its thoughts, if work is neglected today, let it be.

O CAUTIOUS TRAVELLER

(*ORE SABDHANI PATHIK*)

O cautious traveller, roam around for once having lost your way.
Blind your two open eyes with your tears of distress.
The lost heart's bower lies at the frontier of the forgotten path,
Under the thorny trees has fallen the blood-red bunch of flowers,
Creation and destruction play there all day at the infinite ocean's shore.
You sit watching over your long-accumulated savings,
Let them drop, fall off, like the flowers on a stormy night.
Come, now, on your head, wear the victory garland of losing everything.

ETERNAL ME

(*JAKHAN PORBE NA MOR PAYER CHIHNA*)

[Translated by Charu C. Chowdhuri]*

When my footprints will no longer appear on this path,
I will no longer ply my boat over the ferry
When I'll have done with buying and selling
And will have settled my debts and dues
And when my visits to this market will cease,
Never mind if you do not remember me then,
If you do not gaze at the stars and call my name.
When dust will settle on the strings of the lute,
Thorn creepers will climb on the doors of the house,
The garden of flowers will wear a desolate look
With overgrown grass and weeds,
And when on the brinks of the lake moss will gather,
Never mind if you do not remember me then,
If you do not gaze at the stars and call my name.
The flute will play the same tune as it does today on the stage,
Days will pass as they pass now,

---

*Rabindranath Tagore, *Purabi: The East in its Feminine Gender*, trans. by Charu C. Chowdhuri, edited and introduced by Krishna Bose and Sugata Bose, (London, New York, Kolkata: Seagull Books, 2007), pp. 169–70.

Boats will be as heavy-laden at the ferries
And cattle will graze and shepherds play on the field,
Never mind if you do not remember me then,
If you do not gaze at the stars and call my name.
Who is it then who says—on that morning
I will cease to be!
In all the play it will be this me who will play,
By new names I will be called, and
Into new arms I will be pressed,
Yet it will be I who will come and go,
The same eternal me.

ACKNOWLEDGEMENTS

I owe my interest in Tagore translations to my maternal grandfather, Charu Chandra Chowdhuri, who translated a range of Tagore songs and poems into English that were published in the book titled *Purabi: The East in its Feminine Gender*, edited and introduced by my mother Krishna Bose and I. We asked Pramita Mallick, a leading exponent of Tagore's music, to sing eight songs that were included in a CD that accompanied the book.

On the occasion of Tagore's 150th birth anniversary, Pramita Mallick decided to record all his songs composed on his overseas voyages and asked me to translate them for her. These were recorded on a four-CD set titled *Visva Yatri Rabindranath* ('Tagore, the World Voyager'). I read my English translations and provided brief historical contexts of each of the songs, while Pramita Mallick sang the Bengali originals in her enchanting voice. On a fifth CD, titled *Amaar Rabindranath* ('My Tagore'), I recorded readings of translations of ten more songs and sang the originals myself. A request from UNESCO led to my translating another forty songs for the project titled 'Tagore, Neruda, and Césaire for a Reconciled Universal'.

I am grateful to my mother for reading all my translations and helping me strike the right balance between Bengali meaning and English poetry. I thank Jawhar Sircar for his keen interest in reaching Tagore's creativity beyond the boundaries of Bengal and to Chiki Sarkar and Meru Gokhale for helping make this wonderful project a reality.